DOG BREEDS

Border Collies

by Sara Green

Consultant:
Michael Leuthner, D.V.M.
Petcare Animal Hospital
Madison, Wisc.

BLASTOFF!
4
READERS

BELLWETHER MEDIA · MINNEAPOLIS, MN

Note to Librarians, Teachers, and Parents:

Blastoff! Readers are carefully developed by literacy experts and combine standards-based content with developmentally appropriate text.

Level 1 provides the most support through repetition of high-frequency words, light text, predictable sentence patterns, and strong visual support.

Level 2 offers early readers a bit more challenge through varied simple sentences, increased text load, and less repetition of high-frequency words.

Level 3 advances early-fluent readers toward fluency through increased text and concept load, less reliance on visuals, longer sentences, and more literary language.

Level 4 builds reading stamina by providing more text per page, increased use of punctuation, greater variation in sentence patterns, and increasingly challenging vocabulary.

Level 5 encourages children to move from "learning to read" to "reading to learn" by providing even more text, varied writing styles, and less familiar topics.

Whichever book is right for your reader, Blastoff! Readers are the perfect books to build confidence and encourage a love of reading that will last a lifetime!

This edition first published in 2011 by Bellwether Media, Inc.

No part of this publication may be reproduced in whole or in part without written permission of the publisher. For information regarding permission, write to Bellwether Media, Inc., Attention: Permissions Department, 5357 Penn Avenue South, Minneapolis, MN 55419.

Library of Congress Cataloging-in-Publication Data
Green, Sara, 1964–
   Border collies / by Sara Green.
      p. cm. – (Blastoff! readers. Dog breeds)
   Includes bibliographical references and index.
   Summary: "Simple text and full-color photographs introduce beginning readers to the characteristics of the dog breed Border Collies. Developed by literacy experts for students in kindergarten through third grade"–Provided by publisher.
   ISBN 978-1-60014-565-0 (hardcover : alk. paper)
   1. Border collie–Juvenile literature. I. Title.
   SF429.B64G735 2011
   636.737'4–dc22
                                    2010034489

Printed in the United States of America, North Mankato, MN.

010111   1176

Contents

What Are Border Collies?

Border Collies are smart, **athletic** dogs with a lot of energy. The Border Collie **breed** is a member of the **Herding Group** of dogs. Border Collies have an **instinct** to **herd**.

Adult Border Collies are 18 to 22 inches (46 to 56 centimeters) tall at the shoulder. They weigh 27 to 50 pounds (12 to 23 kilograms).

rough
coat

Border Collie **coats** come in many color combinations. The most common is black and white. They can also be **tri-color**, **sable**, and many other color combinations.

Border Collie coats are either smooth or rough. Smooth coats have shorter hair than rough coats.

smooth coat

History of Border Collies

Almost all Border Collies are **descendants** of a **sheepdog** named Old Hemp. He was born near the border of Scotland and England in 1893. This is why his descendants are called Border Collies.

Most sheepdogs herd sheep by nipping at their feet and barking. Old Hemp, however, used slow, stalking movements and his eyes. He could make sheep move with a fierce stare.

Many people preferred Old Hemp's quiet way of herding. They called it giving sheep "eye." People wanted sheepdogs like him.

Old Hemp was the father of many puppies. His puppies were the first Border Collies. Like Old Hemp, they were intelligent dogs that used their eyes and stalking movements to herd.

People saw that Border Collies were strong and independent. They could run long distances without getting tired. They could herd sheep on their own, even when their owners were far away. Soon, farmers in the United States wanted Border Collies to herd their sheep.

Border Collies Today

People who have Border Collies as pets must keep them busy and active. Owners can enter their Border Collies in **sheepdog trials**.

In these trials, dogs herd flocks of sheep. Dogs earn points by moving a flock across a field, through gates, and into a pen.

fun fact

The record for the fastest time in a flyball race is 14.864 seconds. It was set by a team of crossbred dogs that were part Border Collie.

In an activity called **flyball**, Border Collies show off their speed. Two four-dog teams race each other on a course. A dog must jump over four hurdles and push the **flyball box** to shoot a ball into the air. It must retrieve the ball, then jump back over the hurdles before the next dog on its team can start. The fastest team wins!

flyball box

Border Collies also enjoy **disc dog competitions**. In these contests, people throw discs to their dogs over both short and long distances. The dogs earn points when they catch the discs in the air. Dogs get more points for catching discs that fly longer distances. Some dogs do flips as they catch the discs!

! fun fact

Tests have shown that Border Collies are the most intelligent dog breed.

Because of their high energy level, Border Collies need exercise every day. They become restless and sometimes destructive if they do not stay active.

Many people take their Border Collies to **dog parks** to play fetch and meet other dogs. Some people teach their Border Collies tricks. Can you keep up with a Border Collie?

Glossary

athletic—good at activities that require strength, speed, and skill

breed—a type of dog

coats—the hair or fur of animals

descendants—younger family members who are all related to an older family member

disc dog competitions—contests where people throw discs for their dogs to catch in the air

dog parks—places where dog owners can take their dogs to run and play with other dogs

flyball—a relay race for dogs

flyball box—the box at the end of a flyball course; dogs push the flyball box to shoot a ball into the air.

herd—to make people or animals move as a group

Herding Group—a group of dog breeds that move animals from place to place

instinct—a natural way to behave without being taught

sable—a brownish black color

sheepdog—a type of dog that herds sheep

sheepdog trials—events that test a dog's ability to herd sheep

tri-color—having three colors; tri-color dog coats are often black, white, and tan.

To Learn More

AT THE LIBRARY

American Kennel Club. *The Complete Dog Book for Kids*. New York, N.Y.: Howell Book House, 1996.

Jones, Marcia Thornton. *Champ*. New York, N.Y.: Scholastic, 2007.

Stone, Lynn M. *Border Collies*. Vero Beach, Fla.: Rourke Publishing, 2007.

ON THE WEB

Learning more about Border Collies is as easy as 1, 2, 3.

1. Go to www.factsurfer.com.

2. Enter "Border Collies" into the search box.

3. Click the "Surf" button and you will see a list of related Web sites.

With factsurfer.com, finding more information is just a click away.

Index

The images in this book are reproduced through the courtesy of: Eric Isselée, front cover; J. Harrison/
KimballStock, pp. 4-5, 7; Andra_ Cerar, pp. 6, 19 (small); Jon Eppard, p. 8; ARCO/C. Steimer/Age
Fotostock, p. 9; SeanShot, p. 10; Picani Picani/Photolibrary, p. 11; Digital Vision/Getty Images, p. 12
(small); FLPA/Wayne Hutchinson/Age Fotostock, pp. 12-13; clearviewstock, pp. 14-15; Nicky Dronoff-
Guthrie, pp. 16-17, 17 (small); Fibena, pp. 18-19; Juniors Bildarchiv/Age Fotostock, p. 20; Nick Ridley/
KimballStock, p. 21.